C000269514

A COLDNESS

poems by

Jerry T. Johnson

Finishing Line Press
Georgetown, Kentucky

A COLDNESS

Copyright © 2023 by Jerry T. Johnson
ISBN 979-8-88838-291-2 First Edition
All rights reserved under International and Pan-American Copyright Conventions.
No part of this book may be reproduced in any manner whatsoever without written
permission from the publisher, except in the case of brief quotations embodied in
critical articles and reviews.

ACKNOWLEDGMENTS

Blue Moon Literary Art & Review—A Coldness
great weather for MEDIA—Rage And Clamor
Global Poemic—Troubled
Rogue Scholars Press—Fatigued
Barnstorm Journal—I Too Mourn
Three Rooms Press / Maintenant 15—I Awoke In Charlottesville
The Pedestal Magazine—Gun
Drunk Monkeys Literary and Arts Journal—We Sigh
Beyond Words Literary Magazine—Wintry Blues

Publisher: Leah Huete de Maines
Editor: Christen Kincaid
Cover Art: Shutterstock, Royalty-free stock photo ID: 394244926, Standard
license, Contributor: Zabavna
Author Photo: InspiredWordNYC.com
Cover Design: Elizabeth Maines McCleavy

Order online: www.finishinglinepress.com
also available on amazon.com

Author inquiries and mail orders:
Finishing Line Press
PO Box 1626
Georgetown, Kentucky 40324
USA

Table of Contents

*To all my friends in Danbury, Connecticut,
where I wrote most of this poetry chapbook!*

A COLDNESS

during a cruel winter, a frozen
lake seems to whisper: "the worst
is yet to come"

already we erode towards glacial ruin
little sound is heard in the street
icicles shiver in desolate corners
glass chimes tingle chilling tones

parents curl up with trembling
children bitten by bitterness
the storm is bitter, the storm is cold

we weep til we are weep-less
we faint underneath onslaught
of battering upon battering more.
we wait for tomorrow's last rage

and sorely we bleed in today's harsh wintry rain

RAGE AND CLAMOR

football players swinging at delicate heads with metal helmets
soccer fathers swinging hard knocking out virulent soccer moms
middle school basketball coaches decked by screaming mothers
mommy, daddy tantrums explode at a three year old's T-Ball game

vitriol is on sale and the supermarkets are congested
the store greeters are trampled to death shortly after Thanksgiving
another fight erupts over another shopping mall parking space
a skirmish at the clearance rack and a cleanup needed at aisle seven

beltway gridlock once again impedes everybody's progress
civility sends to congress a letter and a bill of resignation
Sumner attempts to roll in his grave my oh my what a pity he can't
Sumner's dust still bruised from that eighteen fifty-six caning

is our national humanity overdosing our rage and clamor?
are epidemics spreading while no physician is monitoring?
is every race, every culture infected with a bile of madness?
are our melting pots seething a gluttony of hatred?

TROUBLED

Pandemic night number
one hundred, twenty-five.
you stir in your sleep.
your eyes pop open.
you look at the clock
sitting on the nightstand.
the time reveals that
you only slept for five
short minutes and now
you are wide awake.
you leave your bed
slowly you walk
down the hall,
your body weary,
your mind overactive,
subconscious troubled.
you make a cup of tea.
no caffeine, no honey,
just warm, black liquid.
steam rises, aroma
wafts through your
troubled space.
midnight arrives.
you sip. you meditate.
calmed. you become.
calmed. you become.

FATIGUED

You stare at yourself in the mirror
Your eyes red, your hair distressed,
You're not smiling, You're fatigued.
You're in the middle of a another
lockdown, another surge,
another day of teleconferences,
one after the other over
and over ad nauseam.
another day of fretting
over politics, another day
of mourning over murders,
another day of hearing
talking heads, another
day of strident division,
another day of children
—fatigued too, at home
all day, all night, all week.

"This is exhausting," you
mutter to yourself. You just
want to remove your face mask
and sit in a room crowded with
a thousand mask-less people
and declare your freedom.
But your common sense
appears and annoys you.
You realize you are in a tsunami.
You realize you must stand down
from errant and misguided notions.
You realize you must let this rage
pass, and deal with the aftermath
and the ruin and the wreckage for
a while and a while and a while.

You sweat from the strain
your rumination, you sit down,
you point the remote at the tube
once again, the news is on and
you hear breaking news:
Vaccination is ninety-five
percent effective. Sunlight
streams through the vent your
curtains. You lift your sorrow
drenched head. Grateful.

EARTH DAY—
a different perspective

Humanity Raises A Fist,
Declares Freedom while
pissing toxin on wearied soil

Earth Awakes in Stockholm.
Awakes from Syndrome
Awakes Abused. Bruised. Sore.

in the middle of winter
bears awake early
from hibernation

in the middle of winter
birds misdirected
fly north

snow falls
across the Equator
in July and August

unabashed
humanity pisses toxin,
toxin, toxin, toxin more.

Earth Awakes in Stockholm,
Earth Awakes from Syndrome,
Ravished, Bruised and Sore.

Nature seems confused,
misdirected. No it isn't.
Earth's not taking the battering.
Anymore.

Earth will have Her Day.

NEW YORK TO CHARLOTTE

My train left Wilmington an half-hour ago
It's four-forty prime meridian, eastern
standard time, daylight is on the wane

Thick clouds murky gray hover lowly
not far away from treetops limbs bare
Winter just arrived four days ago.

It has been ten months since I rode
any sort of train, subway or airplane
Twenty-Twenty. The year of pandemic.

I am mask-less. masks aren't required
in a private room as long as you keep
your door shut. My door is shut.

My room reminds me of my first
train ride in Europe, overnight
Frankfurt, Germany to Prague

That accommodation had a sliding,
glass door also. Curtains you could
close, like my accommodation now.

My steward knocks on my glass door.
It is dinner time. I put on my black
cloth mask, open the door, take

a large white paper bag from her
tell her thanks and off she goes.
I shut my door, go mask-less and eat.

It is well after five now, daylight is gone
I see row houses. We're coming up
on Baltimore. Halfway to destination.

Halfway to my destination. I mull.
over my destiny

I TOO MOURN
—after Langston Hughes

Liberty misunderstood
Liberty misrepresented
Liberty lied on, lied about

wears a veil, dresses
in sackcloth, spreads ash
across her forehead, ashes
across her landscapes torn

Liberty weeps beneath darkness
Liberty gazes upon terror once again
Liberty outraged once again
Liberty overwhelmed falls to the ground

Liberty rises, Liberty stands, Liberty raises her torch

But does Liberty raise her torch for all?
Like Langston, I'm the darker brother
and I Too Sing America, and despite
the fact that Liberty in the harbor

never welcomed me, alongside Liberty

I Too Mourn

I AWOKE IN CHARLOTTESVILLE

another train ride.
a private car due
to COVID Nineteen.
one-forty-five
in the morning
the steward made
my bed. I'm six feet
four inches tall,
I worried but to my
surprise, in my bed
I snugly fit, I laid my
head on my pillow, soon
I drifted into dreamland.

I awoke in Charlottesville

in a postlude of aftermath
of horrid nightmare,
I gazed out my window.
fog and haze walked
up and down the streets
beneath the burning
of the morning's sunshine

I thought about
the Unite the Right
supremacist rally
of twenty-seventeen.
when far-right, alt-right,
right-wing militias,
neo-Nazi, neo-Fascist
neo-Confederate,
Klu-Klux Klansmen,
and violent riot
left fear, injury, death
in bloodlust quake.

Now. outside the window
my private room my train
just shadows of fog and haze,
walking on the streets
beneath rays a sun mourning,
shadows of fog and haze,
shadows fog and haze

soon I will arrive in Washington
D.C. where I will see a Capitol
recently besieged by violence
masquerading freedom.
In time will daylight melt
the haze, the fog, the lies,
the terror, the onslaught,
the murder, the masquerade,
our fears, our tears?

I Awake. I Ask the Conductor.
Are We Yet. Still. Stuck.

In Charlottesville?

GRATEFULNESS!!!

Numb and weary from
driving seven hundred
fifty miles o'er course of
two days. Not in the mood
at the moment for strategies
or tactics or best plans made,
plans well thought out,
thought through, nonetheless
not meandering for this is
a moment—for gratefulness.

despite weariness, despite strain,
contrary to disillusionment,
despite broken heartedness,
despite fracture, in spite of
bruise, though in bitter dispute
with liars, though sad witness
to bloodshed. I take a moment,
this is a moment of Gratefulness.

A BEAUTIFUL AFTERNOON

June First, Twenty, Twenty-One
Danbury, Connecticut
A Beautiful Afternoon.
Outdoors. Seated. A nice table.

The day's heat, yields to coolness.
I'm cool too, relaxed, just chillin.
a blue sky adorned with fluffy clouds
hanging low. speakers mounted,

music piped. horizons. chillin.
House Sparrows dance
with Black-Capped chickadees
on ledges across from my table.

a Great Blue Heron glides overhead
I gaze towards the pond fed by
Miry Brook and Mill River.
Danbury Fair Mall glistens

in the wash of sunlight
the Heron descends,
touches down in the still
green water, stands tall

one legged, then chills.
the Swans turn their heads,
look at the Heron, then resume
their moment, the Geese

obnoxious, as usual, oblivious
to the Heron, the Swan, the Mall
and all, nonetheless, the Geese chill.
I gaze at my mask, long
removed for food and drink.
slowly I sip my club soda.

I Have. A Moment. I Continue. To Chill.

ANOTHER MARTINI

a night of abandon
sipping Jim Beam
poured over a large
slow-melting cube of ice.

pretending to be Hemingway
once again, seated, "in a
clean well-lighted place"

all ain't right wit da world
but this space my current solitude
is alright with me.

a beautiful lady
dressed in black blouse,
black apron, steps up

to the bar service counter
and says, "Another Martini."
the bartender complies.
baring a pleasant smile

she thanks him and walks
off, carrying the martini
and other drinks on the
wide round serving tray

I start writing, pretending
to be Hemingway once again,
seated, "in a clean well-lighted place"

i wonder if Hemingway
wrote at least one line or two
at Sloppy Joes, Duval Street,
Key West or Harry's Bar

in Venice or Hotel Lutetia
in Paris or did he just run
up bar tabs as alleged
by many historians.

funny, I think to myself
i have been to all three
of those hangouts
frequented by Hemingway

and I never wrote one
line of prose or poetry
when I visited those places.

another beautiful lady
dressed in black blouse,
black apron, steps up
to the bar service area

"Another Martini," she says.

I twirl my pen between my
fingers, move my writing pad
closer, press my pen upon
it. *I'm not Hemingway,*

I say to myself, as I write
as I sit "in a clean well-lighted place."

all ain't right wit da world
but this space my current solitude
is alright with me.

PEOPLE WATCHING

seated outside.
a high top table,
a carafe of thick
glass, before me.

the carafe bares
a full litre, still water,
clear shimmer beckoning.

seated outside
a Bistro, Second Ave,
East Eighty-Eighth,
Manhattan.

sipping, watching
traffic: foot traffic,
paw traffic, claw
traffic, four-wheel
traffic. two-wheel
traffic. all moving
rapidly

like red blood cells
speeding through
arteries flowing
to hearts, charging
nerves, awaking
cerebral reflexes.
my cerebral reflexes,
Awaken!

I watch, I listen, I hear,
I feel. I say to myself

Welcome...to New York!

DARK PLACES
—after the movie scene: Frank Has the Blues in Naked Gun 2 ½

I remember being in a dark place.

dark places, dark spaces,
perpetual melancholy.
season after season feels
a long, drawn-out Winter.

when sitting in a dark place
I listen to songs played
on strings that weep.

I nurture my bruise, I feed
myself pity. I nurse whatever's
in the glass standing before me.

I feel like a disaster. I think
about disasters. I think about
the Hindenburg, I think about
the Titanic. I am saddened more.

then I turn from thinking about
serious disasters and I think
about disasters much less severe.

I think about that presidential
campaign of Michael Dukakis
I think about that notorious field
goal attempt by Scott Norwood.

I think about all the songs
alleged written and allegedly
sang by Milli Vanilli.

I pause. Then I think about
the silly and the ridiculous.

I think about ASSORTED
Chia Pets and hoodie pillows

and edible spray paint and
grass flip flops and quack bill
muzzles for dogs and beer
holsters and potato chip
grabbers and condom flash
drives. At this point I'm laughing
at the ridiculousness of it all.

I laugh at the ridiculousness
my own drama, the self-inflicted
kind and the kind inflicted by
circumstance and the kind
inflected by others. I rise,
I pay my tab, I grab my coat,

smiling, I leave my dark place.

GUN

you got a gun
I got a gun
everybody
got a gun

you angry
I angry
everybody
angry

you frustrated
I frustrated
everybody
frustrated

blood in the river
blood in the street
blood in the meadow
blood in the dale
blood in the ocean tide

you got a gun
I got a gun
everybody
got a gun

do we really gotta load it
do we really gotta aim it
do we really gotta fire it

just because
we frustrated
we dejected
we rejected
we starved
we naked
we angry
we alone

WE SIGH

"Our state mourns another life
of a black man taken by law enforcement,"
said the Governor of Minnesota.

Brooklyn Center, a suburb
of Minneapolis. Minneapolis,
not a bridge

but a city of sighs.
"the sun don't shine"
"the moon don't move

the tides" in Trower's time,
nor in yours, nor in mine.
Interrogations

Doge's Palace, the crossing
to Prigioni Nuove, marked
an ending

to summary executions.
but summary executions
pervade crossings

walked by black men.
blood flows in the crossings
blood flows in the rivers

blood flows in the streets
crossed by black men
crossed by black women

and after anguished cries
we bury our summarily murdered
and bearing a heavy melancholy,

We Sigh

LANGSTON'S RIVERS

Earlier today, I saw a T-Shirt
worn by someone, not
of my own race, The T-Shirt
said, "Stop Killing Black People."
I nodded my head towards
her, she nodded back, she
understood my quiet "Bravo!"

Now seated in my desk chair,
headphones on.   Listening to
a dirge of sorrows, flattened,
bruised, red the blood, seeping.

I pause, I listen to Langston's Rivers:
The Nile Weeps, The Euphrates Sobs,
The Mississippi Screams.

I hear Langston's Rivers, ask:
"Why the murders?
Why the rapes?
Why the hangings?"

I hear Emitt Till ask,
"Why? Why? Why?"
I hear Medgar ask,
I hear Martin ask,
I hear Malcolm ask.
They ask, "Is it over?"

I hear Trayvon answer,
I hear Breonna answer,
I hear Eric Gardner answer,
I hear George Floyd answer,
I hear many others answer:
They say, "It's much worse now."

I listen to Langston's Rivers:
The Nile Weeps,
The Euphrates Sobs,
The Mississippi Screams.

Seated my desk chair, headphones on,
Listening, a dirge of sorrows.
We cross our own "bridge of sighs."
We tread our own "trail of tears."
We still live a nightmare.
Nonetheless, we still dream—A Dream!

RED ROPES, YELLOW ROPES, GREEN ROPES

It is the first day of summer.
I'm in Danbury, Connecticut.
I'm taking a morning walk
through the countryside.
Humidity is taking a walk
through the countryside too.
Today's humidity reminds
me the days I marched
Air Force trainees to tech
school at Keesler Air Base
in Biloxi, Mississippi,
mid-August, nineteen
seventy-four, through
muggy noonday suns
beneath haze, sweltering.

We donned stripe-less,
drab-green uniforms
called Fatigues, a word
derived from the late
sixteenth century meaning:
"extra duties of a soldier.
I wore a yellow rope draped
over the left shoulder
my Fatigues, signifying
that I was second in
command my unit.
those who wore green
ropes were third, those
who wore red ropes
were first. Our red rope
leader absent most times
due to much recovering
from many weekend, beach
excursions Panama City,
Florida. Therefore, daily
it was I, who marched
the troops to class.

Our red rope leader did
show up once when a
Four Star General from
Washington visited our base.
Generals from Washington
visiting Keesler Air Base—A BIG DEAL.

Weeks prior his arrival
everyone the base was busy:
painting barracks white,
mending fences, repairing
airplane engines, truck
engines, lawn mower engines,
repairing anything with an
engine, mowing lawns, painting
grass that browned—green.

A parade stage was built
for the General to observe
the squadrons as they marched
to class. Our sunburned,
red-eyed, profusely sweating,
red rope leader asked me what
was he supposed to do. "March
the troops to training class!"
I responded. "Remember.
They taught us how to do
that in Leadership School,"
I added, "You will have to
lead the unit in an 'Eyes Right'
when you step in front of the
General." Our red rope leader
sweated more. Two green ropes
our unit giggled, I glared,
they muted themselves.

Our red rope leader said,
"I've forgotten that.
Actually I've forgotten
most what was taught
in Leadership School."
I felt lips the green ropes
break into a smile, I glared
again, they grimaced.
"Three steps before you
reach the General, issue
the command, 'Eyes
...Right,' turn your head
to the right, raise your
right hand and salute
the General. Keep
your salute until the unit
passes the General, drop
your hand, look forward,
march on.

Can you handle this?"
Our red rope leader froze.
"Tell ya what," I said,
"Lead the unit, turn your
head, salute the General,
I will call the cadence, issue
the command from the
back of the line."
Our red rope leader nodded
agreement, the unit assembled,
two green ropes and I the very
back of the line, optics painfully
amusing, all three of us,
the only African-Americans.

Our red rope leader
called the troops to
ATTENTION. I took it
from there. FORWARD
HARRR...I commanded
and the unit seventy-five
plus trainees moved
forward. We never used
cadence hut, two, three four.
That was perhaps an
Army thing or maybe
it was just a Hollywood thing.
At that time marching orders
issued by Air Force drill
sergeants and squad leaders
were more: a grunt, grunt,
grunt, grunt, than: an hut,
hut, hut...two, three,
four with feet of soldiers
hitting the ground synchronized
with each barked grunt.

after an half mile of marching
the green ropes barked,
"Stop bouncing, you
gonna make the General
dizzy, straighten up."
I kept calling cadence,
from the back, projecting
my voice louder and louder
as we approached the parade
stand, where stood the General,
a music band, other Generals,
and Colonels and Majors,
and Captains and Lieutenants
and Sergeants galore.

Our red rope leader was
just a few steps away from
the General. Projecting
louder, above playing
of the band, I commanded,
"Eyyyes... Right!" In unison,
the unit and our red rope
leader, turned their heads
to the right and raised their
hands up the button line of
their shirts and saluted
the General, who returned
salute, our unit marched by
the General, we lowered our
salute, looked forward, marched on.
We arrived at the tech school,
disassembled, went to class.
Later that night I led the squad
back to our dormitory, our
red rope leader gone again.

At formation the next day,
our red rope leader showed
when our squadron commander
made a special appearance.
Our squadron commander
lauded our red rope leader for his
fine display of military excellence.
the green ropes and I spread
our lips, bearing our teeth wide
in astonished disbelief.

my mind returns to my walk
in Danbury, Connecticut.
Today's humidity in
Danbury isn't as thick
the mugginess Biloxi,
nor am I in the military
any longer. I'm in the
corporate world now.
Nonetheless, one thing
hasn't changed. I still
call cadence from the
back of the line, while
corporate red rope leaders
get to shine before all
the corporate Generals.

WINTRY BLUES
—after Maya Angelou

Autumn Leaves. Fallen.
Still. Dry. Brown.
Silent. Stoic as they
await the wind—or worse,
the leaf blowers.

Soon they meld into
Earth, covered by friendly
snowflakes which paraglide
from peaceful skies gently
landing, spreading into blankets.

Autumn peacefully sleeps.
Only for a moment.
Her blanket soon disturbed
by ice, sent from angry blizzards.

We weep during harsh winters.
In corners we cringe on frigid days.
We hang dark curtains draping
away the sight of frozen limbs.

We dream of monsters
We awake at midnight
doused in sweat. Our saturation
molds. Into Icicles. We Shiver.

We look at our clocks. Alarmed,
we search for calendars.
Finding one we scroll to
Spring. We Long. We Hope.

We Wait. We Anticipate.
But the Time is Now.

We Rise!

Jerry T Johnson is a Poet and Spoken Word Artist whose poetry has appeared in a variety of literary publications worldwide. Jerry is author of 2 poetry collections: *A Coldness* published by Finishing Line Press and *Poets Should Not Write About Politics* published by Evening Street Press. In addition to being the winner of the 2020 Evening Street Press' Sinclair Poetry Prize, Jerry's poetry has also appeared in: *Burning Word Literary Journal, great weather for MEDIA* 2017 & 2020 Anthologies, *The Long Islander* (Walt's Corner), *Straylight Literary Magazine, Here Comes Everyone* (Silhouette Press), *Drunk Monkeys Literature + Film Magazine, Barnstorm Literary Journal, Blue Moon Literary & Art Review, Brownstone Poets 2020 Anthology, Blue Lake Review, ANYDSWPE 2020 Anthology* (RogueScholars Press), *Beyond Words International Literary Magazine, Three Rooms Press, New Note Poetry* and many more. Jerry's poem "The Apology" which appeared in his full-length collection, *Poets Should Not Write About Politics* (Evening Street Press) was nominated for a Pushcart Prize in 2022.

In addition to his published work, Jerry is co-host for great weather for MEDIA's Spoken Word Sundays in New York City. Jerry also serves as host of the Poets, Writers & Storytellers Stage of the annual Norwalk Art Festival in Norwalk, Connecticut. You may follow Jerry's work on the following social media networks: jtjohnpoet.com, twitter.com/jetjohn3 and facebook.com/jtjpoetry.

Milton Keynes UK
Ingram Content Group UK Ltd.
UKHW040108030823
426179UK00003B/54